Setting Personal Boundaries: The Power of Saying No Without Guilt

Overcome People-Pleasing, Manage Your Time, and Reclaim Your Happiness

Alex Monroe

Copyright © 2024 by Alex Monroe

All rights reserved.

No part of this book may be reproduced in any form or by any electronic or mechanical means, including information storage and retrieval systems, without written permission from the author, except for the use of brief quotations in a book review.

Contents

Foreword   v

1. The Power of No – Redefining Boundaries and Taking Control   1
2. People-Pleasing and Its Hidden Costs   8
3. The Art of Assertive Communication   13
4. Time Management for a Balanced Life   19
5. Techniques for Saying No Without Guilt   25
6. Practicing Boundaries in Personal Relationships   32
7. Boundaries in the Workplace   38
8. Transforming Your Mindset: Boundaries as Self-Care   44
9. Tools and Exercises for Boundary Setting   50
10. Afterword   64

Foreword

Saying "no" has always been tricky, hasn't it? For many of us, those two little letters carry the weight of an entire planet's worth of guilt, fear, and awkward smiles. We've all been there: someone asks, "Can you help me move this weekend?" and before you know it, you're nodding enthusiastically, picturing yourself trapped under a couch with a bad back, silently wondering why you can't just say *no*.

If that resonates, you're in the right place. Welcome to *Setting Personal Boundaries: The Power of Saying No Without Guilt*, where we finally tackle the gloriously messy art of setting limits—and do so with a side of humor, because, let's face it, you've got to laugh to keep from crying sometimes.

Here's the thing: today's world is all about doing more, giving more, being more. Society practically hands you a trophy for overextending yourself. "Oh, you're juggling 15 commitments, working late nights, and haven't slept in three days? Wow, you're amazing!" But inside, you're probably a human-shaped puddle of exhaustion, wondering when someone's going to notice you're running on fumes.

Spoiler alert: they're not going to notice. Why? Because you've trained the world to believe you're available 24/7. Saying yes to every

Foreword

request is like sticking a "Please Interrupt My Life" sign on your forehead. Don't worry; I've been there too. For years, I thought saying "yes" made me kind, dependable, and a little bit heroic. Turns out, it just made me *tired*. And cranky. (Just ask my friends—they've got stories.)

This book is the result of my journey from overworked, overcommitted, and overwhelmed to—dare I say it?—balanced. No, I'm not here to pretend I have it all figured out. (I still can't say no to free samples at the grocery store.) But what I *can* say is this: learning to set boundaries has transformed my life. And it can do the same for you.

Throughout these pages, we're going to challenge everything you've been taught about saying no. You'll learn why it's not selfish, why it doesn't mean people will stop liking you, and why it's actually one of the kindest things you can do—for yourself and others. We'll talk about how to handle the guilt, the fear, and those pesky people who just don't take no for an answer. And yes, we'll sprinkle in some case studies of folks who've done the work and lived to tell the tale.

Now, fair warning: this isn't about building walls so high you end up in a self-imposed fortress of solitude. Boundaries aren't about shutting people out; they're about letting the right ones in. They're about choosing how you spend your time, energy, and love. In short, they're about saying yes—but only to the things that truly matter.

So, grab a cup of coffee (or tea, or wine—no judgment), find a cozy spot, and let's dive in. Together, we'll unpack the power of "no" and, with a bit of luck, transform it from a dreaded word into your new favorite tool for happiness.

Because trust me: life's too short to spend it carrying other people's couches.

Here's to setting boundaries—and to saying no with a smile.

Alex Monroe

Chapter 1
The Power of No – Redefining Boundaries and Taking Control

Overview of Boundaries: Building a Framework for Healthy Relationships

Let's start with a simple truth: boundaries are not walls. They're not barriers meant to shut people out or create conflict. Boundaries are, in fact, bridges—they connect us to others in healthier, more balanced ways while protecting our time, energy, and emotional well-being. Think of them as invisible fences: they let people know where your limits are and what's okay (or not) within your personal space.

Boundaries come in many forms. Some are physical: "No, you can't borrow my favorite sweater." Others are emotional: "I appreciate your opinion, but I don't agree." And then there are time-related boundaries: "I can't meet tonight, but I'm free this weekend." The beauty of boundaries is their adaptability; they fit your life, your needs, and your relationships.

Why are they essential? Without boundaries, relationships can become lopsided, draining, or even toxic. Picture your life as a garden. Boundaries are the fence that keeps out weeds (a.k.a. things that drain you) and lets in sunshine and rain (the people and activities that nourish you). Without a fence, everything—good and bad—gets in, and before you know it, you're overrun by obligations, stress, and emotional clutter.

When you set boundaries, you reclaim control. You teach others how to treat you, and more importantly, you show yourself the respect you deserve. Healthy boundaries aren't just about keeping others in check—they're about fostering mutual respect and understanding, the cornerstone of any strong relationship.

Healthy Boundaries	Unhealthy Boundaries
Clearly communicated and respected by others	Poorly defined or not communicated at all
Flexible and adapt to different contexts	Rigid or nonexistent, leading to confusion
Encourage mutual respect and understanding	Can lead to resentment or over-dependence
Protect your time and emotional well-being	Leave you feeling drained or overwhelmed
Allow you to say no without guilt	Trigger guilt or fear of rejection

This diagram provides a quick, clear snapshot of what effective boundaries look like and how they differ from unhealthy ones

Consequences of Over-Commitment: The Hidden Costs of Saying Yes

Ever find yourself saying "yes" out of reflex? Someone asks for a favor, a meeting, or a weekend commitment, and before your brain even processes the request, your mouth has already agreed. For a moment, you feel relief—after all, you avoided that awkward "no." But then reality sets in, and so does the stress.

Over-commitment is like signing up for a marathon every single day. At first, you might manage. But eventually, your mental health, physical energy, and overall happiness pay the price. Here's how over-committing sneaks up on you:

1 Mental Exhaustion: When you're constantly saying yes, your brain is in overdrive, juggling too many tasks and commitments. Decision fatigue sets in, and even small choices—like what to eat for dinner—can feel overwhelming.

2 Time Drain: Time is your most precious resource, and over-committing means you're giving it away freely. Suddenly, there's no time left for yourself, your family, or the things that genuinely bring you joy.

3 Emotional Burnout: Over-commitment often leads to resentment. You start to feel taken advantage of, even though you were the one who said yes. This resentment can erode relationships and leave you feeling isolated.

4 Loss of Identity: When you're always putting others first, your own needs, goals, and desires get buried. You may wake up one day and wonder, "What about me?"

Here's the kicker: over-commitment doesn't just hurt you; it also diminishes the quality of what you can give to others. By trying to be everything to everyone, you end up being less effective, less present, and less fulfilled.

Practical Steps for Recognizing Boundaries

Self-Assessment: Are Your Boundaries Working for You?

To begin setting healthier boundaries, it's crucial to first identify where they're missing or need improvement. Use these reflection questions as a starting point to evaluate your current boundaries and the impact they have on your life:

1 What activities or commitments drain your energy?

   ○ Think about tasks, favors, or interactions that leave you feeling exhausted, frustrated, or resentful. These are often areas where boundaries are too loose or nonexistent.

2 Are there moments when you feel resentment after agreeing to something?

○ Resentment is a red flag. It often signals that you said yes when you wanted to say no. Take note of these situations—they reveal where boundaries need to be strengthened.

3 When was the last time you said no? How did it feel?

○ If you can't remember, it might indicate a pattern of over-commitment. If you do remember, reflect on the emotions you experienced—were you uncomfortable, or did you feel empowered?

4 Do you regularly feel overcommitted or overwhelmed?

○ Examine whether your schedule leaves little room for rest or self-care. Overcommitment is a sign that your time boundaries may need adjustment.

5 Who or what makes you feel obligated to say yes?

○ Identify specific people, environments, or patterns that trigger people-pleasing habits. Awareness is the first step to breaking the cycle.

Myths About Saying No: Breaking the Guilt Cycle

Let's debunk some of the most common myths about saying no—those sneaky little lies that keep us trapped in the people-pleasing cycle.

Myth 1: Saying No is Selfish

Reality check: Saying no isn't about being selfish; it's about self-preservation. You can't pour from an empty cup. By setting boundaries, you ensure you have the energy to give your best to the things that truly matter.

Think about it this way: if you're always saying yes to others, you're inadvertently saying no to yourself. And who deserves your kindness and care more than you?

Myth 2: People Will Dislike You

Ah, the fear of rejection—the kryptonite of people-pleasers everywhere. The truth? Most people respect and admire honesty. When you set boundaries with kindness, you're teaching others that your time and energy are valuable. Sure, a few folks might balk at first, especially if they're used to you saying yes. But those who truly value you will adjust.

Myth 3: Saying No Will Burn Bridges

There's a way to say no without setting the world on fire. It's all about how you communicate. A polite, respectful no doesn't end relationships—it strengthens them. It shows others that you're reliable and honest, not someone who overcommits and underdelivers.

Myth 4: "I Should Be Able to Handle It"

This myth stems from a toxic belief that your worth is tied to how much you can juggle. But guess what? You're not a circus performer. Saying no doesn't mean you're weak; it means you're wise enough to know your limits.

The "No Toolkit"

Sometimes, the hardest part about saying no is finding the right words. The "No Toolkit" provides ready-to-use responses for common situations, helping you decline with confidence and kindness.

Polite but Firm Responses

When you want to say no while maintaining a friendly tone:
- "Thank you for thinking of me, but I have to pass this time."
- "I appreciate the invitation, but I won't be able to make it."
- "I'd love to help, but I'm currently at capacity and can't take this on."

Offering Alternatives

If you want to soften the no by providing a helpful suggestion:

- "I can't take this on, but have you considered asking [Name]?"
- "I'm unable to commit, but I'd be happy to help you brainstorm other options."
- "I'm not available for this, but let me point you to a resource that might help."

Direct but Respectful

When you need to be straightforward while still showing respect:
- "No, I'm not able to do that."
- "I can't take this on right now."
- "That doesn't work for me."

Professional Settings

For declining requests in the workplace:
- "Thank you for bringing this to me, but I don't have the bandwidth to take it on right now."
- "This sounds like an important project, but I'll need to focus on my current priorities."
- "I'd love to assist, but my schedule is fully booked. Can we revisit this later?"

Personal Relationships

For setting boundaries with friends, family, or partners:
- "I know this is important to you, but I need to focus on myself right now."
- "I understand where you're coming from, but I'm not comfortable doing that."
- "I need to say no so I can take care of other responsibilities."

Bonus Tips for Using the Toolkit

- **Pause Before Responding:** Take a moment to consider your answer. Silence gives you time to formulate a response that aligns with your boundaries.
- **Stick to Your No:** Avoid over-explaining. A simple, respectful no is enough.

- **Practice Makes Perfect:** Use these phrases in low-stakes situations to build confidence.

Flowchart for Deciding When to Say No

Title: *Should I Say Yes or No?*
   1 Does this align with my values or goals?
   ○ Yes → Proceed to the next question.
   ○ No → Politely decline.
   2 Do I genuinely have the time and energy for this?
   ○ Yes → Proceed to the next question.
   ○ No → Politely decline.
   3 Is this something I *want* to do, not just feel obligated to do?
   ○ Yes → Consider saying yes!
   ○ No → Politely decline.

Reclaiming Control Through "No"

Saying no is a skill, and like any skill, it takes practice. But once you master it, the results are life-changing. Imagine a life where you only say yes to what aligns with your values, priorities, and goals. A life where your relationships are built on mutual respect, not guilt or obligation. A life where your energy is spent on what truly matters.

That's the power of no. It's not just a word—it's a decision to take control, set boundaries, and live authentically. So, the next time someone asks for your time, energy, or resources, pause. Ask yourself: Does this serve me? Is this aligned with my goals? Do I genuinely want to do this? If the answer is no, say it—with kindness, confidence, and zero guilt.

Because saying no doesn't close doors—it opens the door to a happier, healthier you.

Chapter 2
People-Pleasing and Its Hidden Costs

The Psychology of People-Pleasing

If you've ever felt like your worth is tied to how much you can do for others, you're not alone. People-pleasing is a deeply ingrained behavior for many, often rooted in early life experiences and societal pressures. While it might seem harmless—or even admirable—on the surface, the habit of always putting others first can have profound emotional and psychological consequences.

The Fear of Rejection

At its core, people-pleasing often stems from a fear of rejection. This fear can manifest in thoughts like:
- *"If I say no, they won't like me anymore."*
- *"I don't want to disappoint them."*
- *"What if they stop asking me for help?"*

These fears create a cycle of over-commitment, as you prioritize external validation over your own needs. For many, this behavior starts in childhood, where saying yes or pleasing others was rewarded, while saying no led to disapproval.

The Desire for Approval

People-pleasers often have a strong desire to be liked and accepted. They may believe:
- Their value comes from being helpful or accommodating.
- Saying no equates to selfishness or laziness.
- They must earn their place in relationships by always giving.

Over time, this approval-seeking behavior becomes automatic, making it hard to differentiate genuine kindness from a compulsive need to be agreeable.

The Personal Costs of People-Pleasing

While people-pleasing may seem like a way to maintain harmony, it often leads to significant personal costs.

1. Burnout

When you're constantly saying yes, your to-do list becomes overwhelming. You stretch yourself too thin, neglecting rest and self-care. The result? Emotional and physical exhaustion.

2. Resentment

Saying yes when you want to say no often breeds resentment—toward others and yourself. You might think:
- *"Why don't they ever help me?"*
- *"Why do I always have to do everything?"* Resentment can damage relationships and leave you feeling bitter and unfulfilled.

3. Loss of Self-Identity

By focusing so much on others' needs, you may lose sight of your own. People-pleasing can cause you to:
- Forget your own goals and dreams.
- Struggle to articulate what you truly want.
- Feel disconnected from your authentic self.

4. Anxiety and Stress

Living to meet others' expectations creates a constant state of pressure. The fear of saying the wrong thing or disappointing someone can lead to chronic anxiety and stress, affecting your mental and physical health.

5. Unhealthy Relationships

People-pleasing often attracts those who take advantage of your generosity, creating one-sided relationships. Over time, this dynamic can leave you feeling undervalued and used.

- ☑ Burnout and exhaustion
- ☑ Resentment toward others and yourself
- ☑ Loss of personal goals and identity
- ☑ Chronic anxiety and stress
- ☑ One-sided, unhealthy relationships

The Costs of People-Pleasing

Identifying People-Pleasing Triggers

Recognizing your triggers is the first step to overcoming people-pleasing. These triggers are the specific situations, people, or emotions that push you into over-commitment. Here are some common ones:

1. Authority Figures

Feeling the need to impress bosses, teachers, or mentors often leads to saying yes out of fear of judgment or career repercussions.

2. Close Relationships

Family and close friends can unintentionally pressure you into saying yes. Phrases like "but you're so good at this" or "you always help me" can feel manipulative, even if not intended that way.

3. Guilt-Inducing Statements

Statements like "I really need you" or "You're the only one who can help" play on your fear of being seen as uncaring or unkind.

4. Fear of Conflict

Avoiding potential arguments or disagreements can lead you to agree just to keep the peace.

5. Social Pressure

Cultural norms or societal expectations might make you feel obligated to volunteer, donate time, or participate in activities you don't have the capacity for.

Trigger	Example	How to Address It
Authority Figures	"I can't say no to my boss"	Use assertive but respectful phrases.
Guilt-Inducing Statements	"You're the only one who can help"	Recognize manipulation and politely decline.
Social Pressure	"Everyone else is doing it"	Focus on your priorities and values.

This table categorizes triggers and provides solutions

Breaking the Cycle: Acknowledging Your Triggers

Here's how to start identifying and addressing your people-pleasing patterns:

1 Pause and Reflect: When asked to do something, take a moment before responding. Ask yourself:
- "Do I really want to do this?"
- "Am I saying yes out of obligation or fear?"

2 Keep a Journal: Write down situations where you felt pressured to say yes. Over time, patterns will emerge, helping you pinpoint triggers.

3 Practice Saying No: Start with small, low-stakes situations. As your confidence grows, you can tackle bigger challenges.

Conclusion: From People Pleaser to Empowered

People-pleasing may feel like a safe way to avoid conflict and maintain relationships, but its hidden costs—burnout, resentment, and a loss of self—are too high a price to pay. By understanding the psychology behind it, recognizing your triggers, and taking steps to prioritize your own needs, you can break free from this cycle.

Remember: saying no doesn't make you selfish—it makes you strong. Every time you honor your own needs, you take a step toward a healthier, more balanced life. Embrace the discomfort, because on the other side lies freedom and self-respect. As you move forward, repeat this affirmation: *"I am worthy of love and respect, even when I say no."*

Chapter 3
The Art of Assertive Communication

In many ways, assertive communication is the bridge that takes you from wanting to set boundaries to successfully doing so. For people-pleasers and those who struggle with over-commitment, mastering this skill can be transformative. Assertive communication is not about dominance or aggression; it is about expressing your needs, thoughts, and feelings clearly and respectfully. This chapter will provide you with the tools and techniques to communicate assertively, empowering you to set boundaries without guilt or fear.

What is Assertive Communication?

Assertive communication is the ability to express your thoughts, feelings, and needs openly while respecting the rights of others. It's a balanced communication style, sitting between the extremes of passivity and aggression.

- **Passive Communication:** Often characterized by avoiding conflict and prioritizing others' needs over your own, passive communication can lead to resentment and a sense of being unheard or undervalued.

• **Aggressive Communication:** At the other end of the spectrum, aggressive communication involves pushing your needs at the expense of others, often leading to conflict and damaged relationships.

• **Assertive Communication:** The sweet spot. Assertiveness allows you to stand up for yourself while fostering mutual respect. It's about saying, "I matter, and so do you."

When you communicate assertively, you show confidence and self-respect, encouraging others to value your time and boundaries. This approach fosters healthier, more balanced relationships.

Benefits of Assertive Communication for Boundaries

1 Clear Expression of Needs
Assertive communication ensures your needs and expectations are clearly understood, reducing misunderstandings.

2 Reduced Stress and Resentment
When you communicate assertively, you're less likely to agree to things you don't want to do, minimizing the risk of feeling overburdened or resentful.

3 Strengthened Relationships
Honest, respectful communication builds trust and mutual respect. By being assertive, you create a foundation for stronger personal and professional relationships.

4 Improved Self-Confidence
Each time you communicate assertively, you reinforce your sense of self-worth, boosting confidence in your ability to advocate for yourself.

Setting Personal Boundaries: The Power of Saying No Without Guilt

Key Techniques for Being Assertive

Becoming assertive requires practice and a willingness to step out of your comfort zone. The following techniques will help you build this vital skill:

1. Use "I" Statements

"I" statements allow you to express your feelings and needs without blaming or accusing others. They shift the focus to your experience, making it easier for others to understand your perspective.

- **Example:**

Instead of saying, "You never listen to me!" try, "I feel unheard when I'm interrupted during conversations. I'd appreciate it if we could take turns speaking."

2. Be Specific and Direct

Ambiguity can lead to misunderstandings. When setting boundaries, be specific about what you need and what you cannot do.

- **Example:**

Vague: "I don't think I can take on this task."

Assertive: "I'm unable to take on this task because my schedule is already full."

3. Maintain Calm and Neutral Body Language

Non-verbal cues play a significant role in communication. Ensure your body language aligns with your assertive words.

- **Tips:**
    - Maintain eye contact (without staring).
    - Keep your posture upright and relaxed.
    - Use a calm, steady tone of voice.
    - Avoid fidgeting or crossing your arms defensively.

4. Practice Saying No

Saying no is one of the hardest aspects of assertive communica-

tion, but it's also the most empowering. Practice short, polite ways to decline requests without feeling the need to over-explain.
- **Examples:**
  - "I appreciate the offer, but I'll have to decline."
  - "Thank you for thinking of me, but I can't commit to this right now."
  - "No, I'm not able to do that, but I wish you the best with it."

5. Acknowledge the Other Person's Perspective

Assertiveness isn't about dismissing others' needs. It's about balancing your needs with theirs. Acknowledge their perspective to foster understanding while holding your boundary.
- **Example:**

"I understand that this project is important to you, but I can't take on additional work at the moment."

6. Stay Consistent

People who are accustomed to you saying yes may initially resist when you begin setting boundaries. Stay consistent with your assertive communication to reinforce your commitment to your limits.

Common Challenges and How to Overcome Them

Even with the best techniques, assertive communication can be challenging. Here's how to address some common obstacles:

Challenge 1: Fear of Rejection
- **Why it Happens:** People-pleasers often fear that saying no will lead to rejection or conflict.
- **Solution:** Remind yourself that rejection is not personal. Healthy relationships respect boundaries, and those who react poorly may not have your best interests at heart.

. . .

Challenge 2: Guilt for Saying No
- **Why it Happens:** You may feel guilty because you're used to putting others first.
- **Solution:** Reframe guilt as a signal that you're prioritizing your needs. Remind yourself that self-care is not selfish—it's necessary.

Challenge 3: Pressure to Over-Explain
- **Why it Happens:** You may feel the need to justify your boundaries to gain approval.
- **Solution:** Keep your responses short and confident. You don't owe anyone a detailed explanation.

Challenge 4: Managing Pushback
- **Why it Happens:** Some people may test your boundaries or try to guilt-trip you.
- **Solution:** Stay firm but polite. Use broken-record techniques (repeating your boundary calmly) if someone persists.
- **Example:**

"As I mentioned, I'm unable to take this on. I appreciate your understanding."

Role-Playing Scenarios for Practice

Practicing assertive communication in low-stakes scenarios can build your confidence. Role-play these common situations with a friend or on your own:

1 Declining Social Invitations
- Scenario: A friend invites you to a last-minute gathering, but you're exhausted.
- Response: "I'd love to see you, but I need to rest tonight. Let's plan something another time."

2 Setting Boundaries at Work

○ Scenario: A colleague asks you to help with their workload when you're already overwhelmed.

○ Response: "I understand you're under pressure, but I can't take on extra tasks right now."

3 Managing Family Expectations

○ Scenario: A family member expects you to attend an event you don't want to go to.

○ Response: "I appreciate the invitation, but I won't be able to make it. I hope it goes well!"

Building Confidence Through Small Wins

Start with smaller, less intimidating situations to practice assertive communication. Gradually, as you see positive results, you'll feel more confident in applying these techniques in more challenging scenarios.

Reflection: Assertiveness as Empowerment

Assertive communication is not about confrontation; it's about connection—both with yourself and with others. Each time you express your needs clearly and respectfully, you're reinforcing your value and creating healthier dynamics in your relationships.

Remember, assertiveness is a skill that takes time to develop. Be patient with yourself as you practice, and celebrate each step forward. With consistent effort, you'll find that assertive communication becomes second nature, enabling you to set boundaries confidently and live a more balanced, fulfilling life.

Chapter 4
Time Management for a Balanced Life

Time is one of our most precious and finite resources. Yet, for many of us, it often feels as though there isn't enough to go around. Between work obligations, family responsibilities, social commitments, and personal goals, it's easy to feel overwhelmed. Without clear boundaries and effective time management, we risk burning out, losing focus, and sacrificing what truly matters.

This chapter will guide you through strategies to prioritize your time, say no at work without guilt, and master time management techniques, particularly for entrepreneurs with unique challenges.

Prioritizing What Truly Matters

Effective time management begins with identifying your priorities. What truly matters to you? Answering this question can help you align your commitments with your core values and long-term goals.

1. Assessing Your Commitments

Take a hard look at how you currently spend your time. Create a list of your typical weekly activities and evaluate each one:
- **Is it aligned with my goals?**
- **Does it bring me joy or fulfillment?**
- **Is it essential, or can it be delegated or removed?**

This exercise often reveals how much time is consumed by tasks that don't serve your priorities.

2. The Eisenhower Matrix: A Practical Tool

Use the Eisenhower Matrix to categorize your tasks and determine where your time should go:
- **Urgent and Important:** Tasks that require immediate attention (e.g., meeting a project deadline).
- **Important but Not Urgent:** Tasks that contribute to long-term goals (e.g., planning your career growth).
- **Urgent but Not Important:** Tasks that are time-sensitive but could be delegated (e.g., answering routine emails).
- **Neither Urgent nor Important:** Tasks that drain your time without value (e.g., excessive social media scrolling).

Focus your energy on tasks in the "Important but Not Urgent" quadrant, where proactive work aligns with your priorities.

3. Aligning with Your Values

Time management is not just about efficiency; it's about alignment. Ask yourself:
- What are my top three values (e.g., family, health, career growth)?
- Are my commitments reflective of these values?

Adjust your schedule to devote more time to activities that honor these values.

Setting Personal Boundaries: The Power of Saying No Without Guilt

Strategies for Saying No at Work

Workplace demands can feel overwhelming, especially in environments that reward overcommitment. Learning to say no professionally is a key skill for preserving your time and energy.

1. Set Clear Boundaries Around Work Hours

- Communicate your working hours clearly to colleagues and clients.
- Avoid checking emails or taking calls outside your set hours unless absolutely necessary.
- **Example:**

"I'm happy to help during my working hours, but I won't be available after 6 PM. Let's connect tomorrow to address this."

2. Manage Up: Proactively Communicate Priorities

If your manager assigns tasks that exceed your capacity, address the situation by sharing your current workload and asking for guidance on prioritization.

- **Example:**

"I'm currently focusing on X and Y projects, both of which are due soon. Could we discuss how to prioritize this new task, or should we defer one of the existing projects?"

3. Use the "Not Now, But Later" Approach

When you can't commit immediately but want to keep the door open, frame your no as a postponement.

- **Example:**

"I'd love to help, but I can't take this on until next week. If it can wait, let's revisit it then."

. . .

4. Learn to Delegate

Many professionals struggle to delegate tasks, fearing it may appear as though they're shirking responsibility. However, delegation is a vital skill for effective time management.

• Identify tasks that others can handle.

• Provide clear instructions and trust the person you've delegated to.

Time Management Tips for Entrepreneurs

Entrepreneurs face unique challenges when it comes to time management. The freedom to set your own schedule can quickly turn into an endless workday without boundaries. Here are some techniques tailored to entrepreneurial life:

1. Create a Structured Daily Routine

While flexibility is one of the perks of entrepreneurship, a lack of routine can lead to inefficiency. Design a schedule that includes time for deep work, administrative tasks, and breaks.

2. Set Boundaries with Clients

Entrepreneurs often feel compelled to say yes to every opportunity, fearing the loss of business. However, over-committing can harm your productivity and client satisfaction.

• Be upfront about your availability and timelines.

• Communicate clearly about the scope of work to avoid scope creep.

• **Example:**

"This project sounds exciting. Based on my current workload, I can start on it next Monday and have it completed by the following week. Does that timeline work for you?"

. . .

3. Use Technology to Your Advantage

Leverage tools that streamline time management and reduce repetitive tasks. Popular options include:
- **Project Management Tools:** Trello, Asana, or Monday.com to organize tasks and deadlines.
- **Time Tracking Apps:** Toggl or Clockify to monitor where your time goes.
- **Automation Tools:** Zapier or IFTTT to automate routine tasks like email follow-ups.

4. Protect Time for Strategic Thinking

It's easy to get bogged down in daily operations, but as an entrepreneur, your greatest value lies in strategic decision-making. Block out regular time for long-term planning and creative thinking.

5. Avoid the "Urgency Trap"

Entrepreneurs often feel like every task is urgent. Use prioritization frameworks like the Eisenhower Matrix to distinguish between true emergencies and tasks that can wait.

Practical Exercises for Time Management

1. Conduct a Weekly Time Audit

Spend one week tracking every activity, noting how long it takes. At the end of the week:
- Identify time-wasting activities.
- Adjust your schedule to focus on high-value tasks.

2. Plan Your Day the Night Before

Each evening, write a brief to-do list for the next day. Prioritize tasks based on their importance, and limit your list to three to five key items.

3. Set "No Meeting" Days

If possible, reserve one or two days a week as "no meeting" days to focus on deep work without interruptions.

4. Adopt the 2-Minute Rule

If a task can be completed in less than two minutes, do it immediately instead of letting it clutter your to-do list.

Reflection: The Balance You Deserve

Time management is not about cramming as much as possible into each day. It's about creating space for what truly matters and living in alignment with your values. By setting boundaries, saying no when necessary, and using proven strategies to organize your time, you can achieve a balanced life where your goals, happiness, and well-being take center stage.

Your time is your most valuable asset—guard it fiercely, and use it wisely.

Chapter 5
Techniques for Saying No Without Guilt

Saying "no" is a powerful act of self-respect and boundary-setting, yet for many people, it is accompanied by feelings of guilt and fear. We often worry about disappointing others, being judged, or damaging relationships. However, saying no is not an act of selfishness—it's a necessary tool for maintaining balance, preserving your energy, and prioritizing what truly matters. In this chapter, we'll explore how to overcome guilt, develop effective ways to say no, and tackle the fear of rejection.

"My time is valuable, and it's okay to protect it."

Understanding Guilt and How to Overcome It

Guilt is one of the biggest barriers to saying no. It often arises from deeply ingrained beliefs or societal conditioning that equates selflessness with virtue.

1. Why Does Guilt Arise?
   • **Cultural Norms:** Many cultures glorify self-sacrifice, particularly for caregivers, parents, or professionals, making boundary-setting feel taboo.
   • **Fear of Being Seen as Selfish:** People-pleasers often conflate saying no with neglecting others' needs.
   • **Desire for Approval:** For those who seek validation through pleasing others, declining a request can feel like a personal failure.

2. Reframing Guilt
   Guilt is not inherently bad; it's a signal that you care about how your actions affect others. However, misplaced guilt can lead to overcommitment and resentment. Reframe guilt as a reminder to evaluate your limits rather than a mandate to comply.
   • **Self-Care Isn't Selfish:** Remind yourself that you cannot pour from an empty cup. By saying no, you're preserving your energy for what matters most.
   • **It's Not About Rejection:** Saying no to a task is not the same as rejecting a person. Keep the focus on the request, not the relationship.

3. Guilt-Management Strategies
   • **Pause and Reflect:** When guilt arises, pause and ask yourself, "Is this guilt justified? Or is it based on an unrealistic expectation?"
   • **Practice Self-Compassion:** Treat yourself with the kindness you would offer a friend.
   • **Focus on the Positive Impact:** Consider how saying no allows you to say yes to your priorities and well-being.

Reflection Exercise: Understanding Guilt

o When was the last time I felt guilty for saying no?
　o What belief or fear caused that guilt (e.g., fear of being selfish, disappointing others)?
　o Was my guilt justified, or did I place unrealistic expectations on myself?

"Saying no is an act of self-care, not selfishness."

Polite Yet Firm Ways to Say No

Saying no doesn't have to be confrontational or harsh. With the right language, you can decline a request while maintaining respect and understanding.

1. Direct but Polite Responses
- **"Thank you for thinking of me, but I have to decline."**
- **"I appreciate the offer, but I'm unable to commit to this right now."**

2. Expressing Gratitude Before Declining
Start with gratitude to soften the no. This shows that you value the other person, even if you cannot meet their request.
- **"I'm honored you thought of me, but I'm not able to take this on."**
- **"I really appreciate the opportunity, but I have to pass."**

3. Setting Boundaries with Honesty

Be upfront about your limits to prevent pushback or guilt-tripping.
- **"My schedule is full, so I won't be able to help."**
- **"I need to focus on my priorities right now, so I'll have to say no."**

4. Offering an Alternative (If Appropriate)

Sometimes, offering a solution can show goodwill while maintaining your boundary.
- **"I can't join this time, but let me know about the next opportunity."**
- **"I'm unable to help, but have you considered asking [name]?"**

5. Delaying a Response

If you need time to evaluate a request, avoid agreeing impulsively.
- **"Let me check my schedule and get back to you."**
- **"I'll need to think about this before committing. Can I let you know tomorrow?"**

> *"I can respect others while honoring my own boundaries."*

Overcoming the Fear of Rejection

The fear of rejection often goes hand in hand with guilt. It's natural to worry about how others will perceive us, but letting this fear dictate our actions can lead to over-commitment and resentment.

. . .

Setting Personal Boundaries: The Power of Saying No Without Guilt

1. Recognize That Rejection Is Not Personal

Most people understand that boundaries are necessary. When someone reacts negatively to a no, it often says more about their expectations than your worth.

- **Reframe the Fear:** Remind yourself that a "no" to one request is a "yes" to something more aligned with your values.
- **Accept Imperfection:** You don't need to meet everyone's expectations to be respected or loved.

2. Build Resilience Through Practice

Each time you say no, you reinforce your ability to prioritize your needs. Start small and gradually tackle more challenging situations.

- Practice with low-stakes situations, like declining a flyer from a salesperson.
- Reflect on positive outcomes after setting boundaries, reinforcing your confidence.

3. Manage the Need for Approval

Overcoming the need for external validation requires shifting your focus inward.

- **Affirm Your Worth:** Your value is not determined by how much you do for others.
- **Celebrate Your Wins:** Acknowledge and reward yourself for every successful no.

Case Studies: Boundary-Setting in Action

Let's look at real-life examples of individuals who successfully overcame guilt and fear to set boundaries.

Case Study 1: Maria, the Overcommitted Parent

Maria was a working mother who felt compelled to volunteer for every school event. Saying no felt like letting her children down. After learning to reframe guilt, Maria began declining non-essential commitments. She said, "I'll always support my kids, but I can't do everything." She found that by focusing on fewer events, she could be more present and less stressed.

Case Study 2: James, the People-Pleasing Professional

James had a hard time saying no to his boss, often taking on extra tasks that left him working late. He started practicing assertive communication by discussing his workload openly. When asked to take on another project, James responded, "I'm at capacity with my current tasks. Can we revisit this once I've completed them?" His boss appreciated his honesty and redistributed the work.

Case Study 3: Sarah, the Entrepreneur with Boundaries

Sarah ran a small business and often said yes to clients' demands out of fear of losing them. She started setting clear boundaries by including timelines and scopes in her contracts. When a client requested extra work outside the agreement, Sarah politely declined, saying, "This falls outside our initial scope. I'd be happy to discuss it as a new project." This professionalism earned her respect and improved her workflow.

Setting Personal Boundaries: The Power of Saying No Without Guilt

Style	Example Response	Impact
Passive	"Sure, I'll do it." (even if overburdened)	Leads to burnout, resentment.
Assertive	"I can't take this on right now, but thank you for asking."	Protects time and energy.
Aggressive	"I don't have time for this. Why are you even asking me?"	Damages relationships.

The benefits of assertiveness

Reflection: Saying No as an Act of Self-Respect

Saying no without guilt is not about being dismissive or unkind—it's about valuing your time, energy, and priorities. Remember, each no is a step toward a more balanced, fulfilling life. It's an act of empowerment and self-respect that allows you to show up as your best self in all areas of life.

Start small, practice often, and celebrate your progress. You'll soon find that saying no not only protects your time but strengthens your relationships by fostering mutual respect and understanding.

Chapter 6
Practicing Boundaries in Personal Relationships

Personal relationships are often the most rewarding yet challenging areas to set and maintain boundaries. With family, friends, and partners, emotional ties and expectations can make it difficult to say no, even when it's essential for your well-being. This chapter will explore strategies for setting boundaries with loved ones, recognizing toxic patterns, and managing difficult conversations with confidence and care.

"It's not selfish to protect my peace."

Boundaries with Family, Friends, and Partners

Establishing boundaries in close relationships can feel uncomfortable at first, but it is a critical step in maintaining healthy dynamics. When done with clarity and kindness, boundaries strengthen relationships by fostering mutual respect and understanding.

Setting Personal Boundaries: The Power of Saying No Without Guilt

1. Setting Limits with Family

Family relationships are often steeped in tradition, obligation, and unspoken expectations, making boundary-setting tricky. Common challenges include intrusive behavior, over-dependence, or unsolicited advice.

- **Tactic 1: Define Your Boundaries in Advance**

Reflect on what behaviors you find unacceptable or draining. Examples include frequent unannounced visits or constant pressure to participate in family events.

  - **Example:** "I love seeing you, but I need you to call before dropping by so I can make sure it's a good time."

- **Tactic 2: Use Positive Framing**

Express your needs in a way that shows respect for the other person's feelings.

  - **Example:** Instead of saying, "You're too nosy about my life," say, "I appreciate your concern, but I prefer to handle this in my own way."

2. Establishing Boundaries with Friends

Friendships thrive on mutual support, but they can falter when one person consistently takes more than they give. Boundaries can help maintain a healthy balance.

- **Tactic 1: Address Small Issues Early**

Don't wait for resentment to build. Address concerns as they arise.

  - **Example:** "I love hanging out, but I'm not able to host every time. Could we alternate who picks the venue?"

- **Tactic 2: Be Honest About Your Limits**

Good friends will respect your honesty and appreciate knowing where you stand.

  - **Example:** "I'd love to help, but I don't have the bandwidth for that right now."

"I can be kind and still say no."

3. Setting Boundaries in Romantic Relationships

In partnerships, boundaries are essential for ensuring both individuals feel valued and respected. Without them, relationships can become imbalanced or even toxic.

- **Tactic 1: Communicate Your Needs Early**

Don't assume your partner will automatically know your limits. Discuss your expectations openly.

  - **Example:** "I need some alone time each week to recharge. How can we work that into our schedule?"

- **Tactic 2: Address Repeated Patterns**

If a partner consistently crosses your boundaries, calmly but firmly address the issue.

  - **Example:** "When you check my phone without asking, it makes me feel like my privacy isn't respected. I need us to work on building more trust."

Practical Exercise for Setting Boundaries

- Relationship: _____ (e.g., sibling, friend, partner)
  - What behaviors drain me in this relationship? _____
  - What boundary could address this issue? _____
  - How can I communicate this boundary effectively?

Recognizing Toxic Patterns and Saying No

Not all relationships are healthy, and it's crucial to recognize when boundaries are not just helpful but necessary. Toxic patterns can include manipulation, guilt-tripping, or repeated boundary violations.

Setting Personal Boundaries: The Power of Saying No Without Guilt

1. Red Flags in Relationships

- **Manipulative Behaviors:** Subtle or overt attempts to control your actions, often framed as "for your own good."
  - **Example:** "If you really cared about me, you'd do this for me."
- **Constant Criticism:** Undermining your confidence to make you feel dependent.
  - **Example:** "You're always so sensitive. Can't you take a joke?"
- **Boundary Resistance:** Refusal to respect your limits or frequent testing of your boundaries.
  - **Example:** Ignoring your request to avoid certain topics or behaviors.

2. Saying No to Toxic Behaviors

When faced with toxic patterns, saying no becomes a form of self-protection.

- **Tactic 1: Be Firm and Direct**

Don't leave room for negotiation when dealing with manipulative individuals.
  - **Example:** "I'm not comfortable with this, and I won't participate."
- **Tactic 2: Limit Engagement**

Minimize interactions with individuals who consistently drain your energy or violate your boundaries.
  - **Example:** "I need to take some space from this relationship to focus on my well-being."

"I deserve relationships that respect my limits."

Communicating Without Conflict

Difficult conversations about boundaries don't have to escalate into conflict. Using calm, clear, and assertive communication can help you navigate these discussions effectively.

Situation	Don't Say	Do Say
A friend invites you to an event	"I can't believe you'd expect me to come!"	"I appreciate the invite, but I can't make it this time."
A partner criticizes your boundaries	"You never respect my needs!"	"When you ignore my boundary, I feel disrespected. Let's work on this together."

Effective and ineffective communication styles compared

1. Stay Calm and Neutral

When emotions run high, it's easy to fall into defensive or aggressive communication. Practice staying calm, even if the other person reacts emotionally.

- **Tip:** Pause before responding to avoid saying something you might regret.

2. Use "I" Statements

Frame your boundary as your need rather than a critique of the other person's behavior.

- **Example:** Instead of saying, "You're always interrupting me," say, "I feel unheard when I'm interrupted. Can we take turns speaking?"

3. Acknowledge Their Feelings Without Backtracking

Validate the other person's emotions while holding firm to your boundary.

• **Example:** "I understand that you're disappointed I can't help, but I need to stick to my commitments."

4. Offer Compromises When Appropriate

When possible, offer alternatives to show goodwill without compromising your limits.

• **Example:** "I can't join this weekend, but let's plan a coffee date next week."

Reflection: Strengthening Your Relationships

Healthy boundaries are the foundation of thriving personal relationships. They ensure your needs are met without compromising your values or well-being. While setting boundaries may feel awkward or uncomfortable at first, with practice, it becomes a natural and empowering part of your interactions.

> *"Setting boundaries shows respect for myself and the people I care about."*

Boundaries are not walls—they are bridges that connect you to others in a way that respects and values both parties. When you set limits with clarity and care, you create space for deeper, more meaningful connections that honor your time, energy, and emotional health.

Take the first step today: reflect on one personal relationship where you need to set a boundary and start crafting a plan to communicate it. You'll find that saying no can be one of the most loving things you do—for yourself and those around you.

Chapter 7
Boundaries in the Workplace

Boundaries in the workplace are essential for maintaining productivity, mental health, and job satisfaction. Yet, in professional settings, the pressure to overcommit or overperform often makes setting boundaries feel risky. However, clear and respectful workplace boundaries not only protect your time and energy but also enhance your credibility and relationships with colleagues.

This chapter will help you establish professional boundaries with confidence, provide actionable strategies for saying no to additional workload, and share inspiring case studies of professionals who reclaimed their peace of mind through boundary-setting.

Professional Boundaries for Peace of Mind

Workplace boundaries are guidelines that help you balance your responsibilities, manage your time effectively, and maintain a healthy work-life balance. These boundaries define what you are willing to do—and not do—in your professional role.

. . .

Setting Personal Boundaries: The Power of Saying No Without Guilt

1. Types of Workplace Boundaries
- **Working Hours:** Define when you are available for work and when you are not. This includes limiting after-hours communication unless there's an emergency.
  - **Example:** "I'm available between 9 AM and 5 PM. Any emails sent after that time will be addressed the following day."
- **Task Limitations:** Know your job description and avoid taking on tasks that fall outside your role unless it aligns with your goals or professional growth.
  - **Example:** "I'd love to help, but this task seems outside my scope. Would you like me to suggest someone else who can assist?"
- **Colleague Interactions:** Set clear expectations for communication styles, meeting frequencies, and acceptable behaviors in the workplace.
  - **Example:** "I'm happy to discuss this during work hours, but I'd prefer we avoid texting about work over the weekend."

2. Why Workplace Boundaries Matter
- **Prevent Burnout:** Constantly saying yes can lead to stress, fatigue, and reduced job satisfaction.
- **Boost Productivity:** Clear boundaries help you focus on high-priority tasks without being distracted by unnecessary requests.
- **Enhance Professional Relationships:** When others understand your limits, they are more likely to respect your time and effort.

How to Say No to Extra Workload Without Jeopardizing Your Job

Saying no at work can be daunting, especially when you fear negative consequences. However, assertive and respectful communication ensures that you set boundaries without appearing uncooperative.

. . .

1. Assess the Request Before Responding

Before agreeing to additional work, evaluate its urgency, alignment with your role, and impact on your current workload.

- **Questions to Ask Yourself:**
  - Does this task align with my priorities and responsibilities?
  - Do I have the time and resources to handle it effectively?
  - Will this task compromise my ability to meet existing deadlines?

2. Use the "Yes, But" Technique

This technique allows you to acknowledge the request while highlighting your limitations.

- **Example:** "Yes, I'd be happy to help, but my current project deadline is Friday. If this can wait until next week, I can take it on."

3. Offer Alternatives

If you can't take on the task, suggest another solution, such as delegating to a colleague or adjusting deadlines.

- **Example:** "I'm unable to take this on right now, but perhaps [Colleague] could assist, or we could extend the deadline to ensure quality work."

4. Set Clear Expectations with Your Manager

If you're frequently overloaded, discuss your workload openly with your manager to find a solution.

- **Example:** "I'm currently managing X and Y projects, and adding another task could impact my ability to meet deadlines. How should we prioritize these tasks?"

5. Be Firm but Respectful

If a request is unreasonable, politely decline without overexplaining.

• **Example:** "I'm afraid I can't commit to this due to my current workload. I hope you understand."

Case Studies: Success Stories of Professionals Who Set Boundaries

Case Study 1: Jane, the Overwhelmed Marketing Manager

Jane was frequently asked to take on extra assignments outside her job description. After attending a time management workshop, she began setting boundaries by assessing her workload and practicing assertive communication. When asked to handle an urgent task, she responded:

• "I'd like to help, but my plate is full this week. Can we schedule this for next week, or would you like me to recommend someone else?"

Her manager appreciated her honesty, and the task was reassigned, allowing Jane to focus on her priorities.

Case Study 2: Mark, the Team Player in IT

Mark prided himself on being a team player but often found himself burned out from saying yes to every request. When his manager assigned him yet another project, he scheduled a one-on-one meeting to discuss his workload.

• Mark explained, "I'm currently working on three high-priority tasks, and taking on another would impact my ability to deliver quality work. Can we revisit this after I complete my current projects?"

His manager not only deferred the new project but also praised Mark for his proactive communication.

Case Study 3: Priya, the Client-Focused Entrepreneur

As a freelance graphic designer, Priya often felt pressured to accommodate last-minute client requests. She started including clear boundaries in her contracts, stating her availability and response times. When a client demanded revisions over a weekend, Priya replied:

- "Thank you for your feedback. I'll begin working on these revisions on Monday and have them ready by mid-week as per our agreement."

This reinforced her professionalism and ensured her personal time remained protected.

Practical Tips for Maintaining Boundaries at Work

1 Set Up Time Blocks

Use your calendar to block out time for focused work and make it visible to colleagues.

2 Avoid Over-Explaining

Keep your responses concise and professional when declining requests.

3 Communicate Proactively

Regularly update your team or manager about your workload to avoid last-minute surprises.

4 Automate Communication

Use email autoresponders to indicate your working hours and expected response times.

Reflection: Creating a Healthy Work Environment

Boundaries in the workplace are not just about protecting your time—they are about fostering a culture of respect and professionalism. By communicating your limits clearly and consistently, you

Setting Personal Boundaries: The Power of Saying No Without Guilt

empower yourself and others to focus on what truly matters, reducing stress and increasing efficiency.

Take a moment to reflect on your current workplace boundaries. Are they serving you, or do they need adjustment? Choose one area where you can set or reinforce a boundary this week and practice saying no with confidence.

Remember, setting boundaries is not a sign of weakness or lack of commitment—it's a sign of self-respect and professionalism that benefits both you and your workplace.

Chapter 8
Transforming Your Mindset: Boundaries as Self-Care

Many people view boundaries as barriers to connection or acts of selfishness. However, boundaries are not walls—they are bridges to a healthier, more fulfilling life. By setting clear limits, you are prioritizing your well-being and creating space for what truly matters. This chapter explores how boundaries are a profound act of self-care, offers techniques for reshaping your mindset about saying no, and invites you to envision the life you can create when you embrace boundaries.

Self-Care Through Boundaries

Setting boundaries is one of the most compassionate things you can do for yourself. It protects your time, energy, and emotional health, allowing you to thrive in both personal and professional relationships.

1. Boundaries Are Not Selfish

Many people-pleasers struggle with guilt when setting boundaries, fearing they'll disappoint others or be perceived as uncaring.

Setting Personal Boundaries: The Power of Saying No Without Guilt

The truth is, boundaries allow you to give your best to others while preserving your own well-being.

- **Why It's Self-Care:**

When you honor your limits, you prevent burnout, reduce stress, and create time for rest, hobbies, and relationships that energize you.

- **Reframe Selfishness:**

Selfishness is taking from others without giving back. Boundaries, on the other hand, ensure you have the capacity to contribute meaningfully to others without depleting yourself.

2. Benefits of Self-Care Through Boundaries

- **Emotional Well-Being:** Boundaries reduce resentment and feelings of being taken advantage of.
- **Time for What Matters:** Clear limits allow you to focus on your values, goals, and loved ones.
- **Improved Relationships:** Healthy boundaries create mutual respect and reduce conflict.
- **Example:**

Saying no to a weekend commitment you're too exhausted to attend might disappoint a friend momentarily, but it allows you to rest and show up as a better version of yourself for future interactions.

Reframing Thoughts on No

The word "no" is often perceived as negative or final, but it can be a powerful act of self-empowerment when framed differently. By reshaping your mindset, you can view saying no as an act of kindness—to yourself and to others.

1. Recognize No as a Positive Choice

Saying no doesn't mean rejecting a person—it means choosing what aligns with your needs and priorities.

• **Reframe Example:** Instead of thinking, "I'm letting them down," think, "I'm being honest about what I can handle."

2. Replace Negative Beliefs with Positive Affirmations

• **Negative Belief:** "Saying no makes me selfish."

o **Reframe:** "Saying no allows me to preserve my energy for what truly matters."

• **Negative Belief:** "People won't like me if I say no."

o **Reframe:** "People who respect me will understand and value my honesty."

3. Practice Saying No Without Guilt

• **Techniques to Try:**

o Use neutral language: "I'm unable to commit to this right now."

o Avoid over-apologizing: "Thank you for asking, but I can't take this on."

o Remind yourself: Saying no doesn't require justification beyond your limits.

• **Quick Exercise:**

Write down three recent situations where you said yes when you wanted to say no. For each, imagine how saying no would have benefited your well-being. This practice helps you internalize the value of no.

Setting Personal Boundaries: The Power of Saying No Without Guilt

Visualizing a Healthier Future

To embrace boundaries fully, it helps to visualize the positive changes they can bring. By imagining a life where your time and energy are protected, you can anchor your boundary-setting efforts in a clear vision of what you want to achieve.

1. Imagine Your Ideal Life with Boundaries
- **Prompt:** Close your eyes and think about your daily life with healthy boundaries in place.
  - How do you feel waking up, knowing you've prioritized your needs?
  - What relationships have improved because you've communicated your limits?
  - How much time do you have for self-care, hobbies, or goals?
- **Write It Down:** Create a journal entry describing a day in your life with strong boundaries. Be specific: What does your schedule look like? How do you respond to requests? What has changed for the better?

2. The Ripple Effect of Boundaries
Healthy boundaries impact every area of your life. By protecting your time and energy, you can:
- **Excel Professionally:** Focus on meaningful work and avoid burnout.
- **Build Stronger Relationships:** Enjoy connections based on mutual respect.
- **Achieve Personal Goals:** Pursue hobbies, health, or education without constant overcommitment.
- **Example:**
Imagine saying no to an extra project at work. The time you reclaim allows you to attend your child's soccer game, go for a

relaxing walk, or read a book you've been putting off. The positive effects ripple into your emotional well-being and relationships.

3. Envision the Cost of No Boundaries

While it's important to focus on the positive, consider what happens if you continue to lack boundaries:

- How does constant overcommitment affect your health, happiness, and relationships?
- What important goals are delayed or abandoned because of saying yes too often?

By visualizing these costs, you can solidify your commitment to creating and maintaining boundaries.

Practical Exercise: A Week of Boundary Practice

To help you put these concepts into action, try this week-long boundary-setting challenge:

- **Day 1-2:** Identify one area of your life where boundaries are lacking (e.g., work, family, friends). Write down how it's impacting you.
- **Day 3-4:** Choose one boundary to implement. Plan how you will communicate it and anticipate potential pushback.
- **Day 5-6:** Practice saying no in a low-stakes situation, such as declining an invite or delegating a task. Reflect on how it felt.
- **Day 7:** Evaluate your progress. How did setting this boundary improve your week? What did you learn about yourself?

Reflection: Boundaries as a Gift to Yourself

Boundaries are not a sign of weakness or selfishness—they are an act of self-love and self-respect. By protecting your time and energy, you are saying yes to what truly matters: your well-being, your goals, and

Setting Personal Boundaries: The Power of Saying No Without Guilt

your relationships. Embracing boundaries doesn't just transform your mindset; it transforms your life.

Remember, every time you say no to something that drains you, you're saying yes to something that fulfills you. Keep practicing, stay patient with yourself, and trust in the process. Boundaries are the foundation of a balanced, joyful, and empowered life.

Chapter 9
Tools and Exercises for Boundary Setting

Setting boundaries is a skill, and like any skill, it improves with practice. While understanding the importance of boundaries is crucial, putting them into action requires confidence, clarity, and persistence. This chapter equips you with practical tools and exercises to help you take that next step—from understanding boundaries to living them.

Through guided activities, you'll learn to build assertiveness, practice saying no, and create a personalized boundary plan tailored to your unique needs. Reflection questions and journal prompts will encourage you to evaluate your progress, celebrate your wins, and address any challenges along the way. By the end of this chapter, you'll not only have a deeper understanding of your boundaries but also a clear roadmap to integrate them into your daily life with confidence and ease. Let's get started on your journey to becoming a boundary-setting expert!

Setting Personal Boundaries: The Power of Saying No Without Guilt

Practical Exercises to Build Confidence in Saying No

Building confidence in setting boundaries and saying no takes practice. The following exercises are designed to help you strengthen your assertiveness, refine your communication skills, and feel more at ease setting limits. These activities range from role-playing scenarios to reflective techniques that you can apply in real life.

1. Role-Playing Scenarios

Role-playing is an excellent way to rehearse saying no in a safe, controlled environment. Grab a friend, family member, or coworker to practice with—or even practice in front of a mirror.

How to Do It:

1 Choose a common scenario where you struggle to say no.

2 Write down the request and your response.

3 Role-play both sides of the conversation. Your partner can act as the person making the request.

Example Scenarios:

• **Workplace:** Your manager asks you to stay late, but you've already committed to an evening with your family.

  o Response: "I understand this is important, but I've made personal plans I can't change. Can we look at an alternative solution?"

• **Social Circle:** A friend invites you to a party, but you're too tired to attend.

  o Response: "Thanks for the invite, but I'm going to pass this time. Let's catch up soon, though!"

Goal: Practice delivering your no with a calm tone, clear body language, and polite phrasing.

2. The "Sandwich" Technique Practice

The sandwich technique helps you deliver a no while cushioning it with positivity and appreciation. It's great for maintaining relationships while setting boundaries.

How to Do It:

1 Start with something positive or appreciative.

2 Deliver your no in the middle.

3 End with an alternative or goodwill.

Example:

- "I really appreciate you thinking of me for this project. However, I'm at capacity right now and won't be able to take it on. Let me know if there's another way I can support you."

Exercise: Write three "sandwich" responses to requests you've struggled with in the past. Rehearse them out loud.

3. The Mirror Method

Practicing in front of a mirror helps you focus on your tone, body language, and confidence while saying no.

How to Do It:

1 Stand in front of a mirror.

2 Practice saying no to a few sample requests, watching your body language and tone.

3 Adjust your posture to be upright and relaxed, maintain eye contact (with yourself), and ensure your tone is calm but firm.

Sample Phrases to Practice:

- "No, I'm not able to do that right now."
- "I appreciate you asking, but I have to decline."
- "Thank you for thinking of me, but I'll need to pass."

Goal: Build self-assurance by visually reinforcing your confidence.

4. The "No Journal"

Keep a journal to track situations where you said no and reflect on the experience.

Setting Personal Boundaries: The Power of Saying No Without Guilt

How to Do It:

1 Each time you say no, write down:
- The situation.
- How you felt before, during, and after.
- The other person's reaction.
- Any lessons you learned.

2 Review your entries weekly to observe patterns, celebrate progress, and refine your techniques.

Example Entry:
- **Situation:** Declined a coworker's request to cover their shift.
- **How I Felt:** Nervous at first, but relieved after.
- **Their Reaction:** They understood and didn't push back.
- **Lesson:** Saying no wasn't as scary as I thought!

5. The 3-Second Rule

The 3-second rule helps you pause and collect your thoughts before responding to a request. This prevents impulsive yeses.

How to Do It:

1 When someone makes a request, take a deep breath and count to three before responding.

2 Use filler phrases to buy time if needed:
- "Let me think about that."
- "Can I get back to you on this?"

3 Decide whether the request aligns with your priorities before answering.

Practice Exercise:

Ask a friend or family member to make mock requests during a conversation, giving you opportunities to pause and think before responding.

6. "Rewrite the Script" Exercise

This exercise helps you reframe past situations where you said yes when you wanted to say no.

How to Do It:

1 Think of a situation where you wish you had set a boundary.

2 Write down the original request and your response.

3 Rewrite the scenario, imagining how you could have said no confidently.

Example:

- **Original Request:** "Can you take on this extra project for me?"
- **Original Response:** "Sure, I'll figure it out."
- **Rewritten Response:** "I'm already at capacity, so I can't take on additional work right now."

7. The Boundary Script Builder

Use this exercise to create scripts for common scenarios where you need to say no.

How to Do It:

1 Identify common requests or situations where you struggle with boundaries.

2 Build a short script using this structure:

- **Step 1:** Acknowledge the request or show appreciation.
- **Step 2:** Clearly state your boundary or say no.
- **Step 3:** Offer an alternative, if appropriate, or express goodwill.

Example Script for Family:

- **Step 1:** "I love how much our family gatherings mean to everyone."
- **Step 2:** "But I need to limit my time to two hours today because I have other commitments."
- **Step 3:** "Let's make sure to plan a longer catch-up next time."

Setting Personal Boundaries: The Power of Saying No Without Guilt

. . .

8. The "Boundary Muscle" Challenge

Strengthening your boundary-setting "muscle" takes practice. Start small and work up to more challenging situations.

How to Do It:

1 For one week, focus on saying no to small, low-stakes requests (e.g., declining a flyer, refusing a second helping of food).

2 Gradually tackle higher-stakes situations, like declining additional tasks at work or saying no to a demanding friend.

3 Reflect on each experience: Did it feel easier over time? How did others react?

Goal: Build confidence progressively, one step at a time.

9. Partner Practice: Boundary Role-Swapping

Practice with a partner where you alternate roles as the requestor and the responder.

How to Do It:

1 The requestor makes a range of realistic requests, from simple (e.g., "Can you lend me your pen?") to complex (e.g., "Can you work late for me tonight?").

2 The responder practices saying no in different ways while maintaining composure.

3 Switch roles and discuss how it felt to be on both sides of the interaction.

10. Daily Affirmations for Assertiveness

Boost your confidence with positive affirmations about your ability to set boundaries.

How to Do It:

1 Write down or repeat daily affirmations like:
- "I have the right to say no without guilt."

- "My needs are just as important as anyone else's."
- "Setting boundaries is a form of self-care and self-respect."

2 Post these affirmations where you can see them daily (e.g., on your mirror or desk).

By consistently practicing these exercises, you'll develop the skills and confidence to set boundaries and say no with clarity and grace. Remember, assertiveness is like a muscle—the more you use it, the stronger it becomes!

Creating Your Own Boundary Plan

Establishing a clear, personalized boundary plan is an essential step in integrating boundaries into your daily life. This exercise will guide you through outlining your personal goals, identifying specific boundaries, and creating a strategy to implement them effectively. A boundary plan acts as a roadmap, helping you navigate challenging situations with confidence and consistency.

Step 1: Define Your Personal Goals

Boundaries are most effective when they align with your values and goals. Start by identifying what you want to protect or prioritize in your life.

Exercise: Reflect on Your Goals

1 Take 10 minutes to list your personal and professional goals.
- What are your top priorities (e.g., health, family, career, hobbies)?
- What activities bring you joy and fulfillment?
- Where do you feel the most stress or overwhelm?

Example Goals:
- Spend quality time with family without work interruptions.
- Maintain a consistent self-care routine.

Setting Personal Boundaries: The Power of Saying No Without Guilt

• Focus on professional growth without overcommitting to unnecessary tasks.

Step 2: Identify Specific Boundaries You Need

Once you've clarified your goals, determine the boundaries that will help you achieve them. Think about areas where you feel drained, overextended, or taken advantage of.

Exercise: Pinpoint Your Boundaries

• Use these categories to brainstorm specific boundaries:
  ○ **Time:** Protecting your time from unnecessary demands.
  ○ **Emotional Energy:** Limiting interactions with toxic or draining individuals.
  ○ **Workload:** Saying no to tasks that don't align with your priorities.
  ○ **Personal Space:** Ensuring you have time and space to recharge.

Worksheet Example:

Area	Boundary Needed	Reason
Time	No work emails after 6 PM	To create work-life balance
Emotional Energy	Limit time with a critical relative to 30 minutes	To reduce stress and anxiety
Workload	Decline projects outside my job description	To focus on my key responsibilities
Personal Space	One evening per week for self-care	To recharge and maintain mental health

Worksheet Example

Step 3: Develop Your Strategy

With your boundaries in mind, outline how you'll communicate, implement, and maintain them. A strong strategy includes clear communication, preparation for pushback, and regular self-reflection.

1. Communicating Your Boundaries

Prepare phrases or scripts to express your boundaries assertively and respectfully. Tailor them to different situations.

Example Scripts:
- **Work:**
  - "I'm unable to take on additional tasks right now, but let's revisit this after I complete my current projects."
- **Friends:**
  - "I value our time together, but I need to leave by 8 PM tonight to get enough rest."
- **Family:**
  - "I love spending time with you, but I need to set a limit on how long we discuss [stressful topic]."

2. Handling Pushback

Not everyone will immediately accept your boundaries. Plan how to handle resistance calmly and firmly.

Strategies for Pushback:
- **Repeat Your Boundary:** Use the "broken record" technique by calmly restating your boundary without justifying it.
  - Example: "As I mentioned, I can't take this on right now. I hope you understand."
- **Validate but Stay Firm:** Acknowledge their feelings while holding your ground.
  - Example: "I understand this is frustrating for you, but I need to prioritize my well-being."

. . .

Setting Personal Boundaries: The Power of Saying No Without Guilt

3. Monitor and Adjust Your Boundaries

Boundaries are not set in stone; they may need to evolve as your circumstances change.

Reflection Questions:
- Are my boundaries helping me achieve my goals?
- Do I feel less stressed and more in control of my time?
- Are there any boundaries that need to be strengthened or revised?

Step 4: Create Your Personalized Boundary Plan

Use the following template to create your plan:

1. My Goals:

Write down three to five key goals you want your boundaries to support.
- Example: "Protect my weekends for personal time and hobbies."

2. My Boundaries:

List specific boundaries to achieve these goals.
- Example: "No work-related calls or emails on weekends."

3. Communication Strategy:

Write sample scripts or responses for common situations.
- Example: "I'm happy to discuss this on Monday during work hours."

4. Handling Challenges:

Plan how you'll address resistance or guilt.
- Example: "If someone pushes back, I'll repeat my boundary calmly and remind myself why it's important."

5. Evaluation Plan:

Decide how and when you'll review your boundary plan.
- Example: "I'll journal weekly about how my boundaries are working and adjust as needed."

Step 5: Practice in Real Life

Once your boundary plan is complete, start small by implementing one or two boundaries in low-stakes situations. Gradually apply more boundaries as your confidence grows.

Daily Challenge:
- Practice one boundary from your plan each day for a week.
- Reflect on the results: How did it feel to assert yourself? How did others respond?

Reflection: Empowering Yourself Through Boundaries

Creating a boundary plan empowers you to take control of your time, energy, and relationships. It's not just about protecting yourself—it's about designing a life that aligns with your values and priorities. With a clear strategy and consistent practice, you'll find that setting boundaries becomes second nature, leading to greater balance, fulfillment, and peace of mind.

Reflection Questions and Journal Prompts: Exploring Progress and Recognizing Achievements

Reflecting on your journey of setting boundaries is essential for recognizing growth, identifying areas for improvement, and staying motivated. Use these questions and prompts to deepen your understanding of your progress and celebrate your achievements. Set aside time each week or month to journal and track your experiences.

Reflection Questions
1 General Progress
- What boundaries have I successfully implemented in the past week/month?
- How did setting these boundaries make me feel?

Setting Personal Boundaries: The Power of Saying No Without Guilt

- What positive changes have I noticed in my life since I started setting boundaries?

2 Challenging Moments
- Was there a situation where I struggled to set or maintain a boundary?
- What made it challenging, and how did I handle it?
- What could I do differently next time to uphold my boundary with confidence?

3 Emotional Impact
- How do I feel when others respect my boundaries?
- How do I manage guilt or fear when I say no?
- What has setting boundaries taught me about self-care and self-respect?

4 Relationships
- How have my relationships changed since I began setting boundaries?
- Are there any relationships where I need to adjust or strengthen my boundaries?
- How can I continue to communicate my boundaries effectively in these relationships?

5 Personal Growth
- What have I learned about myself through this process?
- How has setting boundaries helped me align my life with my values and goals?
- What boundary-setting skill do I feel most proud of mastering?

Journal Prompts
1 Celebrate Wins
- Write about a recent time when you successfully set a boundary. How did it feel? How did others respond?

○ List three things you've accomplished because you protected your time or energy with boundaries.

2 Reframe Challenges
  ○ Reflect on a time when someone resisted your boundary. How did you handle it? What can you learn from the experience?
  ○ Write about a situation where saying yes felt easier than saying no, but reflect on how you could approach it differently next time.

3 Visualize Your Ideal Life
  ○ Imagine your life with strong, consistent boundaries in place. What does your day look like? How do you feel emotionally, physically, and mentally?
  ○ Write a letter to your future self, describing how your commitment to boundary-setting has transformed your life.

4 Track Progress
  ○ At the end of each week, journal about:
    - One boundary you successfully upheld.
    - One situation where you struggled.
    - One strategy you'll try next week to improve.

5 Gratitude for Boundaries
  ○ Write about how boundaries have helped you feel more in control of your time and energy.
  ○ List five ways setting boundaries has improved your relationships, work-life balance, or self-esteem.

Monthly Reflection Exercise: The Boundary Check-In

At the end of each month, conduct a comprehensive review of your boundary-setting progress. Use these prompts:

- **What worked well?** Write about the boundaries that were respected and had the biggest impact on your well-being.
- **What needs adjustment?** Reflect on boundaries that weren't fully upheld or need refinement.
- **How have I grown?** Identify ways you've become more assertive, confident, or aligned with your values.

- **What's my next step?** Set one new boundary-related goal for the coming month.

Why Reflection Matters

Taking the time to reflect on your boundary-setting journey allows you to celebrate your wins, learn from your challenges, and stay motivated. Journaling these experiences not only helps you track your progress but also reinforces your commitment to living a balanced, fulfilling life where your needs are respected. Make reflection a regular part of your boundary-setting routine—it's a powerful tool for growth and self-awareness.

Chapter 10
Afterword

Congratulations on completing this journey! By exploring the principles of boundary-setting, learning to say no, and embracing assertive communication, you have taken meaningful steps toward reclaiming your time, energy, and happiness. Each chapter in this book has equipped you with tools to navigate the complexities of relationships, work demands, and self-care with confidence and clarity.

Saying no is not just about setting limits—it's about honoring your values, respecting yourself, and creating space for what truly matters. It's an act of empowerment, a declaration that your needs and priorities are valid. As you've seen throughout this book, setting boundaries is not selfish; it's a profound expression of self-respect and self-love.

A Lifelong Practice

Boundary-setting is not a one-time event; it's an ongoing process. There will be moments when it feels easy and moments when it feels challenging. You may encounter resistance from others or struggle with guilt, but every effort you make strengthens your ability to live authentically and with intention. Remember, boundaries are like muscles—the more you practice, the stronger and more natural they become.

Be patient with yourself as you continue to grow. Celebrate your successes, learn from setbacks, and always remind yourself of why you started this journey. The power of boundaries lies in their ability to transform your life over time, helping you to prioritize joy, peace, and purpose.

Visualizing Your Empowered Future

Take a moment to imagine the life you are building with these tools. Picture a day where you confidently say no without fear of judgment or guilt. Envision relationships built on mutual respect, where your boundaries are valued and reciprocated. See yourself thriving in a career where your time and talents are appreciated, not taken for granted. Most importantly, visualize the sense of fulfillment and balance that comes from living in alignment with your values.

This is the life you are creating—one step, one boundary, and one choice at a time.

Your Next Steps

As you close this book, commit to practicing what you've learned. Start small: say no to something minor today or reaffirm a boundary you've already set. Over time, these actions will become second nature, and you'll find that the effort was worth it.

You've already taken a bold step by seeking to change how you approach boundaries. Trust in your ability to continue this journey. You have the tools, the knowledge, and the courage to create the balanced, fulfilling life you deserve.

A Final Reminder

Boundaries are not just about keeping things out—they're about making room for what truly belongs in your life. Every time you set a boundary, you are affirming your worth and choosing a path toward greater joy and peace. You hold the power to shape your life, and that power begins with the simple yet transformative act of saying no.

Thank you for letting this book be a part of your journey. Go forward boldly, empowered by the knowledge that your time, energy, and happiness are worth protecting. The life you envision is within your reach—one boundary at a time.